AMISH FOODS

EAT LIKE THE AMISH WITH AUTHENTIC AMISH RECIPES

By
BookSumo Press
Copyright © by Saxonberg Associates
All rights reserved

Published by
BookSumo Press, a DBA of Saxonberg Associates
http://www.booksumo.com/

ABOUT THE AUTHOR.

BookSumo Press is a publisher of unique, easy, and healthy cookbooks.

Our cookbooks span all topics and all subjects. If you want a deep dive into the possibilities of cooking with any type of ingredient. Then BookSumo Press is your go to place for robust yet simple and delicious cookbooks and recipes. Whether you are looking for great tasting pressure cooker recipes or authentic ethic and cultural food. BookSumo Press has a delicious and easy cookbook for you.

With simple ingredients, and even simpler step-by-step instructions BookSumo cookbooks get everyone in the kitchen chefing delicious meals.

BookSumo is an independent publisher of books operating in the beautiful Garden State (NJ) and our team of chefs and kitchen experts are here to teach, eat, and be merry!

INTRODUCTION

Welcome to *The Effortless Chef Series*! Thank you for taking the time to purchase this cookbook.

Come take a journey into the delights of easy cooking. The point of this cookbook and all BookSumo Press cookbooks is to exemplify the effortless nature of cooking simply.

In this book we focus on Amish. You will find that even though the recipes are simple, the taste of the dishes are quite amazing.

So will you take an adventure in simple cooking? If the answer is yes please consult the table of contents to find the dishes you are most interested in.

Once you are ready, jump right in and start cooking.

— BookSumo Press

TABLE OF CONTENTS

About the Author 2

Introduction 3

Table of Contents 4

Any Issues? Contact Us 7

Legal Notes 8

Common Abbreviations 9

Chapter 1: Easy Amish Recipes 10

    Sunny Cornbread 10

    Creamy Noodles and Beef Casserole 12

    Homemade Amish Noodles 14

    Whipped Lemon Tart 16

    Crisco and Buttermilk Cookies 18

    Tartar Tart 20

    Fluff Cookies 22

    Nutty Brownies 24

    Ritz Chicken Bake 26

    Creamy Cheese Spread 29

    Warm Lima Salad 31

    Herbed Chicken Stuffing 33

    Creamy Velveeta Bake 35

    Crunchy Beet Salad 37

- Apple Pie Brownies 39
- Fairies Cake 41
- Roasted Pasta Stew 43
- Tropical Jell-O Salad 45
- Cheesy Potato Casserole 47
- Coconut Pudding 49
- Rolled Walnuts Tart 51
- Allspice Tart 53
- Glazed Crisco Puffs 55
- Valentine Strawberry Amish Bread 57
- Spicy Orange Bread 59
- Poppy Bread 61
- Splenda Muffins 63
- Nutty Carrot Muffins 65
- Juniper Stir Fry 67
- Hot Cornmeal 69
- Green Stew Pan 71
- Creamy Jell-O and Egg Salad 73
- Chicken Farm Soup 75
- Creamy Chicken Roast 77
- Applesauce Muffins 79
- Vanilla Coffee Cake 81
- Banana Cake with Vanilla Frosting 83
- Vanilla Blondies 86
- Amish Mint Tea 88

Crunchy Broccoli with Cheddar Sauce ... 90

Peanut Crackers ... 92

Sweet and Salty Beef Chili ... 94

THANKS FOR READING! JOIN THE CLUB AND KEEP ON COOKING WITH 6 MORE COOKBOOKS.... ... 96

Come On... ... 98

Let's Be Friends :) ... 98

Any Issues? Contact Us

If you find that something important to you is missing from this book please contact us at info@booksumo.com.

We will take your concerns into consideration when the 2nd edition of this book is published. And we will keep you updated!

— BookSumo Press

LEGAL NOTES

ALL RIGHTS RESERVED. NO PART OF THIS BOOK MAY BE REPRODUCED OR TRANSMITTED IN ANY FORM OR BY ANY MEANS. PHOTOCOPYING, POSTING ONLINE, AND / OR DIGITAL COPYING IS STRICTLY PROHIBITED UNLESS WRITTEN PERMISSION IS GRANTED BY THE BOOK'S PUBLISHING COMPANY. LIMITED USE OF THE BOOK'S TEXT IS PERMITTED FOR USE IN REVIEWS WRITTEN FOR THE PUBLIC.

Common Abbreviations

cup(s)	C.
tablespoon	tbsp
teaspoon	tsp
ounce	oz.
pound	lb.

*All units used are standard American measurements

Chapter 1: Easy Amish Recipes

Sunny Cornbread

Ingredients

- 1 C. sifted flour
- 1/4 C. sugar
- 1 tbsp baking powder
- 3/4 tsp salt
- 1 C. yellow cornmeal
- 1 egg, well beaten
- 1 C. milk
- 5 tbsp shortening, melted and cooled

Directions

- Before you do anything, preheat the oven to 425 F. Grease a loaf pan and place it aside.
- Get a large mixing bowl: Stir in it the flour with sugar, baking powder, salt and cornmeal.
- Get another mixing bowl: Whisk in it the milk with egg and shortening.
- Mix in the flour mix until they become smooth. Pour the batter into the loaf pan and cook it in the oven for 22 min.
- Allow the cornbread to sit for 5 min in the pan then place it aside to lose heat completely and serve it.
- Enjoy.

Servings Per Recipe: 4

Timing Information:

Preparation	10 mins
Total Time	30 mins

Nutritional Information:

Calories	473.1
Fat	20.8g
Cholesterol	61.4mg
Sodium	767.0mg
Carbohydrates	63.5g
Protein	9.2g

* Percent Daily Values are based on a 2,000 calorie diet.

Creamy Noodles and Beef Casserole

Ingredients

- 1 lb. ground beef
- 1 onion, chopped
- 1/2 C. celery, chopped
- 1 tbsp garlic, minced
- 1 (14 oz.) cans diced tomatoes
- 1 (10 1/2 oz.) cans cream of chicken soup
- 1 (12 oz.) packet wide egg noodles
- 1/2 C. shredded cheddar cheese

Directions

- Before you do anything, preheat the oven to 350 F. Grease a casserole dish and place it aside.
- Bring a large pot of water with a pinch of salt to a boil. Prepare in it the noodles according to the directions on the package.
- Place a large pan over medium heat Brown in it the beef with onion for 4 min. Stir in the celery with garlic and cook them for 6 min.
- Lay half of the noodles in the bottom of the casserole dish. Drain half of the beef mix and spread it over it.
- Lay on top half of the tomato followed by half of the soup and half of the cheese. Repeat the process to the remaining ingredients to make another layer of them.
- Place the casserole in the oven and let it cook for 1 h. Serve it hot.
- Get a large mixing bowl:
- Enjoy.

Servings Per Recipe: 4

Timing Information:

| Preparation | 25 mins |
| Total Time | 1 hr 25 mins |

Nutritional Information:

Calories	737.5
Fat	29.9g
Cholesterol	169.7mg
Sodium	894.6mg
Carbohydrates	76.5g
Protein	39.7g

* Percent Daily Values are based on a 2,000 calorie diet.

Homemade Amish Noodles

Ingredients

- 2 1/2 C. all-purpose flour
- 1 tsp salt
- 2 eggs, beaten
- 1/2 C. milk
- 2 tbsp butter, melted
- 1 drop yellow food coloring

Directions

- Get a large mixing bowl: Combine in it the flour with salt. Mix in it the egg with milk, butter and food coloring.
- Knead the dough with your hands or a stand mixer for 6 min until it becomes soft. Cover it with a kitchen towel and let it rest for 12 min.
- Transfer the dough to a lightly floured surface. Use a rolling to flatten the dough until it becomes 1/4 inch thick.
- Slice into long strips and place them aside to rest for a few minutes.
- Bring a large salted pot of water to a boil. Cook in it the pasta until it becomes soft then serve it.
- Enjoy.

Servings Per Recipe: 4

Timing Information:

Preparation	
Total Time	

Nutritional Information:

Calories	390.5
Fat	10.0g
Cholesterol	112.5mg
Sodium	684.0mg
Carbohydrates	61.2g
Protein	12.2g

* Percent Daily Values are based on a 2,000 calorie diet.

Whipped Lemon Tart

Ingredients

- 3 oz. lemon pudding mix
- 1 oz. Knox unflavored gelatin
- 1 C. granulated sugar
- 2 1/4 C. water
- 2 tbsp lemon juice
- 3 egg yolks
- 1 tsp grated lemon rind
- 1 tbsp butter, melted
- 3 egg whites
- 1 C. Cool Whip
- 1 9-inch baked pie crust

Directions

- Place a heavy saucepan over medium heat: Stir in it pudding mix, gelatin, sugar, 1/4 C. water and lemon juice.
- Mix in the egg yolks with the rest of the water. Heat them through while stirring all the time. Stir in the butter with lemon rind and turn off the heat to make the filling.
- Get a large mixing bowl: Cream in it the egg whites until their soft peaks.
- Pour the filling into a mixing bowl after it cools down for a while. Fold into it the egg white.
- Pour the filling into the pie shell and place it in the in the fridge to sit for 1 h.
- Once the time is up, cream the cool whip and use a piping bag to garnish the pie with it. Place it back in the fridge until ready to serve.
- Enjoy.

Servings Per Recipe: 8

Timing Information:

| Preparation | 15 mins |
| Total Time | 20 mins |

Nutritional Information:

Calories	336.0
Fat	13.2g
Cholesterol	74.6mg
Sodium	308.7mg
Carbohydrates	48.7g
Protein	6.8g

* Percent Daily Values are based on a 2,000 calorie diet.

Crisco and Buttermilk Cookies

Ingredients

- 2 C. sugar
- 1 C. Crisco
- 4 large eggs
- 4 tsp vanilla extract
- 4 C. flour
- 4 tsp baking powder
- 2 tsp baking soda
- 1 tsp salt
- 1 C. buttermilk

Directions

- Before you do anything, preheat the oven to 425 F. Line up a baking sheet and place it aside.
- Get a large mixing bowl: Beat in it the sugar and Crisco until they become light. Mix in the eggs gradually.
- Fold the vanilla into the mix and place it aside.
- Get another mixing bowl: Stir in it the flour, baking powder, baking soda and salt. Fold it in the eggs batter with buttermilk gradually.
- Use a round spoon to drop mounds of dough in the cookie sheet. Place it in the oven and let them cook for 7 min.
- Place the cookies aside to lose heat completely then serve them.
- Enjoy.

Servings Per Recipe: 1

Timing Information:

Preparation	15 mins
Total Time	25 mins

Nutritional Information:

Calories	938.3
Fat	38.6g
Cholesterol	142.6mg
Sodium	1140.6mg
Carbohydrates	133.5g
Protein	14.1g

* Percent Daily Values are based on a 2,000 calorie diet.

Tartar Tart

Ingredients

- 1 C. white sugar
- 2 tbsp flour
- 1 egg, beaten
- 1 C. molasses
- 2 C. water
- 1 tsp vanilla
- 2 C. flour
- 1 C. brown sugar
- 1 tsp baking soda
- 1 tsp cream of tartar
- 1/4 C. butter
- 1/4 C. shortening
- 2 9-inch pie shells, unbaked

Directions

- Before you do anything, preheat the oven to 350 F.
- Place a heavy saucepan over medium heat: Stir in it the white sugar, 4 Tbsp flour, egg, molasses, water, and vanilla.
- Cook them until it starts boiling. Turn off the heat and place the mix aside to lose heat for a while to make the filling.
- Get a large mixing bowl: Stir in it 2 C. flour, brown sugar, baking soda, cream of tartar, butter, and shortening. Mix them well until you get a crumbly mix.
- Divide the filling between the 2 pie shells. Sprinkle the crumble mix over them. Place the tarts in the oven and let them cook for 44 to 46 min.
- Place the aside to cool down completely. Place the tarts in the fridge until ready to serve.
- Enjoy.

Servings Per Recipe: 1

Timing Information:

Preparation	20 mins
Total Time	1 hr

Nutritional Information:

Calories	3198.7
Fat	114.8g
Cholesterol	166.7mg
Sodium	1916.9mg
Carbohydrates	521.2g
Protein	28.6g

* Percent Daily Values are based on a 2,000 calorie diet.

FLUFF COOKIES

Ingredients

- 2 large egg yolks
- 1 1/2 C. sugar
- 2/3 C. milk
- 1 (1 oz.) package unflavored gelatin
- 1/2 C. cold water
- 2 egg whites
- 1 C. cream, whipped
- 3 tbsp butter
- 3 tbsp brown sugar, packed
- 12 graham crackers

Directions

- Place a heavy saucepan over medium heat: Whisk in it the milk with sugar and egg yolks. Let the mixture cook until it becomes slightly thick.
- Get a small mixing bowl: Stir in the cold water with gelatin. Mix it into the hot mixture. Place the aside to cool down until it become thick.
- Get a large mixing bowl: Beat in it the egg whites until their soft peaks.
- Get another mixing bowl: Beat in it the cream until it soft peaks.
- Fold the egg white with cream into the egg yolk mixture after it cools down.
- Get a large mixing bowl: Combine in it the butter, brown sugar and crackers well.
- Spread half of the mix in the bottom of a lined up casserole dish. Spread over the cream then sprinkle the remaining crumbs mix on top.
- Place the casserole in the fridge for at least 4 or an overnight. Slice it into squares then serve it.
- Enjoy.

Servings Per Recipe: 12

Timing Information:

| Preparation | 20 mins |
| Total Time | 25 mins |

Nutritional Information:

Calories	251.5
Fat	11.0g
Cholesterol	62.3mg
Sodium	88.7mg
Carbohydrates	35.1g
Protein	4.4g

* Percent Daily Values are based on a 2,000 calorie diet.

Nutty Brownies

Ingredients

- 4 oz. baking chocolate squares
- 1 C. butter, softened
- 2 C. sugar
- 4 large eggs, beaten
- 2 tbsp vanilla
- 1 dash salt
- 1 C. flour
- 2 C. chopped nuts

Directions

- Before you do anything, preheat the oven to 350 F. Grease a baking pan and place it aside.
- Place a heavy saucepan over medium heat. Stir in it the butter with chocolate until they melt.
- Turn off the heat. Mix into them the rest of the ingredients. Pour the mixture into the pan.
- Place it in the oven and let it cook for 22 min. Allow it to cool down completely then slice it into squares and serve it.
- Enjoy.

Servings Per Recipe: 24

Timing Information:

Preparation	10 mins
Total Time	30 mins

Nutritional Information:

Calories	341.8
Fat	25.6g
Cholesterol	51.3mg
Sodium	167.7mg
Carbohydrates	30.1g
Protein	6.4g

* Percent Daily Values are based on a 2,000 calorie diet.

Ritz Chicken Bake

Ingredients

- 1 loaf pan cornbread, crumbled (8x8-inch)
- 6 slices bread, crumbled
- 1/4 lb. Ritz crackers or 1/4 lb. saltine crackers, crumbled
- 1/2 C. butter or 1/2 C. margarine
- 1 C. coarsely chopped onion
- 1 C. coarsely chopped celery
- 2 tsp bell seasoning (or other chicken seasoning with a thyme and sage type mixture)
- salt and pepper, to taste
- 4 1/2 C. chicken broth (or broth made from a whole chicken, approximate measure, see recipe)
- 4 eggs, beaten
- 1/2 C. milk
- 1/2 tsp baking powder
- 3 -4 C. diced cooked chicken (or the meat from one whole chicken, about 4 to 4 1/2 lbs., cooked with water and seasonings to make)
- 3/4 C. dried cranberries (optional)

Directions

- Place a large pot of water over high heat and bring it to a boil. Place in it the chicken and let it cook for 1 h with your favorite seasoning.
- Drain the chicken and reserve the broth. Remove the meat from the bones and cut it into bite size pieces.
- Before you do anything, preheat the oven to 425 F.
- Get a large mixing bowl: Stir in it the cornbread, bread, and crackers. Place it aside.
- Place a large pan over medium heat. Heat the butter in until it melts. Sauté in it the celery with onion for 5 min.

- Add them to the cornbread mix with bell seasoning, a pinch of salt and pepper. Drizzle over them some broth to and mix them until they become slightly moist.
- Mix in it the eggs with milk into them. Add enough broth until you get a slushy mix.
- Stir in the diced chicken. Pour the mix into a greased casserole dish. Place it in the oven and let it cook for 20 to 30 min. Serve it warm.
- Enjoy.

Servings Per Recipe: 8

Timing Information:

| Preparation | 25 mins |
| Total Time | 1 hr 55 mins |

Nutritional Information:

Calories	387.4
Fat	22.7g
Cholesterol	177.7mg
Sodium	863.9mg
Carbohydrates	22.4g
Protein	22.3g

* Percent Daily Values are based on a 2,000 calorie diet.

Amish Foods

Creamy Cheese Spread

Ingredients

- 3 1/2 C. water
- 4 C. milk
- 2 1/2 tsp baking soda
- 5 lbs. white processed cheese or 5 lbs. yellow American cheese

Directions

- Place a heavy saucepan over medium heat: Heat in it the milk with water until they start boiling.
- Stir in the cheese with baking soda until they melt. Use a hand whisk to whisk them until they become creamy.
- Serve your spread with some bread or over a salad.
- Enjoy.

Servings Per Recipe: 1

Timing Information:

Preparation	15 mins
Total Time	25 mins

Nutritional Information:

Calories	4054.5
Fat	303.4g
Cholesterol	975.5mg
Sodium	16165.7mg
Carbohydrates	111.4g
Protein	224.6g

* Percent Daily Values are based on a 2,000 calorie diet.

Warm Lima Salad

Ingredients

- 1 lb. lima beans
- 4 potatoes, diced
- 2 oz. ham, cubed
- 1 1/4 C. half-and-half cream
- 1 tbsp butter
- 1/4 C. chopped parsley
- 1 tsp grated nutmeg

Directions

- Place a large pot over medium heat. Stir in it the potato with beans. Pour over them enough water to cover them.
- Cook them until they start boiling. Lower the heat and let them cook for 22 min.
- Discard the water. Stir the ham, half and half, butter, parsley and nutmeg into the pot. Season them with some salt and pepper.
- Serve your salad warm.
- Enjoy.

Servings Per Recipe: 4

Timing Information:

| Preparation | 5 mins |
| Total Time | 30 mins |

Nutritional Information:

Calories	393.6
Fat	13.1g
Cholesterol	43.0mg
Sodium	572.6mg
Carbohydrates	56.1g
Protein	14.5g

* Percent Daily Values are based on a 2,000 calorie diet.

Herbed Chicken Stuffing

Ingredients

- 2 lbs. white bread, cut in cubes
- 2 lbs. chicken thighs, Poached
- 1/2 C. parsley, Minced
- 3/4 C. onion, Chopped
- 1 C. celery, Chopped
- 1 C. carrot, Shredded
- 1 1/4 C. potatoes, boiled, chopped
- 1 tbsp rubbed sage
- 1 tbsp celery seed
- 1 tsp dried thyme
- 1/2 tsp black pepper
- 1/2 tbsp turmeric
- 5 eggs
- 12 oz. evaporated milk
- 2 1/2 C. homemade chicken broth

Directions

- Before you do anything, preheat the oven to 350 F. Grease a casserole dish and place it aside.
- Spread the bread cubes on 2 baking sheets. Place them in the oven and bake them for 16 min.
- In the meantime, discard the chicken bones and skin then shred the meat.
- Get a large mixing bowl: Stir in it the toasted bread with the shredded chicken, chopped veggies and seasonings.
- Get another mixing bowl: Whisk in it the eggs with broth and milk. Add them to the bread mix and combine them well.
- Cover the bowl and let it sit for 1 h. Once the time is up, pour it into the casserole dish.
- Place the pan in the oven and let it cook for 1 h. Serve it warm.
- Enjoy.

Servings Per Recipe: 20

Timing Information:

Preparation	0 mins
Total Time	0 mins

Nutritional Information:

Calories	306.6
Fat	11.5g
Cholesterol	89.8mg
Sodium	465.0mg
Carbohydrates	33.7g
Protein	16.0g

* Percent Daily Values are based on a 2,000 calorie diet.

Creamy Velveeta Bake

Ingredients

- 1 C. Spam, diced
- 1 C. elbow macaroni
- 1/2 lb. Velveeta cheese
- 1 C. unseasoned breadcrumbs
- 2 C. frozen peas
- 3 tbsp flour
- 3 tbsp butter
- 2 C. milk
- 1/2 tsp salt
- 1/2 tsp pepper

Directions

- Before you do anything, preheat the oven to 425 F. Grease a casserole dish and place it aside.
- Prepare the macaroni according to the directions on the package cooking for half of the recommended time only.
- Place a heavy saucepan over medium heat: Stir in it the four with butter. Add to them the milk while mixing all the time.
- Stir into it half of the Velveeta cheese until it completely melts to make the white sauce.
- Stir the spam with cooked macaroni and the white sauce in the casserole dish. Place it in the oven and let it cook for 46 min. Serve it hot.
- Enjoy.

Servings Per Recipe: 4

Timing Information:

Preparation	15 mins
Total Time	1 hr

Nutritional Information:

Calories	696.7
Fat	41.7g
Cholesterol	123.9mg
Sodium	2158.6mg
Carbohydrates	51.3g
Protein	29.1g

* Percent Daily Values are based on a 2,000 calorie diet.

Crunchy Beet Salad

Ingredients

- 1 cooked beet, sliced
- 4 heads curly endive lettuce, washed, sliced
- 2 tsp parsley, chopped
- 2 tsp tarragon, chopped
- 2 tsp chervil, chopped
- 1/4 tsp salt
- 1/8 tsp black pepper, ground
- 3 tbsp olive oil
- 1 1/2 tbsp wine vinegar

Directions

- Get a serving bowl: Lay in it the lettuce then top it with the beets, sprinkle with parsley, tarragon, and chervil.
- Add to them the olive oil with vinegar, a pinch of salt and pepper. Mix them well. Serve your salad right away.
- Enjoy.

Servings Per Recipe: 4

Timing Information:

| Preparation | 30 mins |
| Total Time | 30 mins |

Nutritional Information:

Calories	185.9
Fat	11.2g
Cholesterol	0.0mg
Sodium	269.2mg
Carbohydrates	19.1g
Protein	6.9g

* Percent Daily Values are based on a 2,000 calorie diet.

Apple Pie Brownies

Ingredients

- 1 C. butter, softened
- 1 3/4 C. sugar
- 2 eggs, well beaten
- 1 tsp vanilla
- 2 C. flour
- 1 tsp baking powder
- 1 tsp baking soda
- 1 tsp cinnamon
- 1/2 tsp salt
- 2 C. baking apples, peeled and chopped
- 1/2 C. walnuts

Directions

- Before you do anything, preheat the oven to 350 F. Grease a baking pan and place it aside.
- Get a large mixing bowl: Beat in it the butter, sugar, eggs and vanilla until they become slight and smooth.
- Mix into it the flour with baking powder, baking soda, cinnamon, and salt.
- Fold the walnuts with apples into the batter. Pour it into the greased pan. Cook the brownies in the oven for 46 min.
- Allow the brownie pan to cool down completely then cut into squares and serve it.
- Enjoy.

Servings Per Recipe: 9

Timing Information:

Preparation	20 mins
Total Time	1 hr 5 mins

Nutritional Information:

Calories	508.0
Fat	26.1g
Cholesterol	101.2mg
Sodium	471.2mg
Carbohydrates	65.2g
Protein	5.5g

* Percent Daily Values are based on a 2,000 calorie diet.

Fairies Cake

Ingredients

- 10 eggs
- 1/2 tsp cream of tartar
- 1 dash salt
- 1 tbsp water
- 3/4 C. cake flour
- 1 C. sugar
- 1 tsp vanilla

Directions

- Before you do anything, preheat the oven to 350 F. Grease a cake pan and place it aside.
- Get a large mixing bowl: Mix in it the egg whites with a hand mixer until they become light.
- Mix in it the cream of tartar and beat them until their soft peaks.
- Get a mixing bowl: Cream in it the egg yolks and salt. Mix in the water gradually followed by the sugar until its soft peaks.
- Stir the flour with egg whites into the egg yolk batter. Pour it into the cake pan and cook it for 42 min in the oven.
- Allow it to cool down completely then serve it with your favorite toppings.
- Enjoy.

Servings Per Recipe: 10

Timing Information:

Preparation	25 mins
Total Time	1 hr 5 mins

Nutritional Information:

Calories	189.6
Fat	5.0g
Cholesterol	211.5mg
Sodium	85.8mg
Carbohydrates	28.5g
Protein	7.1g

* Percent Daily Values are based on a 2,000 calorie diet.

Roasted Pasta Stew

Ingredients

- 1/4 C. beef bouillon granules
- 10 C. hot water
- 3 lbs. boneless chuck roast, trimmed
- 8 whole cloves
- 3 celery ribs, chopped
- 2 large carrots, peeled, chopped
- 1 large onion, quartered
- 1 seeded green bell pepper, quartered
- 1 bunch parsley sprig, plus
- 1/2 C. parsley, chopped
- 2 bay leaves
- 1/2 tsp ground pepper
- 1 (16 oz.) packages egg noodles
- 1 tsp salt
- freshly-ground pepper

Directions

- Before you do anything, preheat the oven to 350 F. Grease a casserole dish and place it aside.
- Get a large oven proof pot. Stir in it the beef bouillon with water. Stir into them the chuck roast, cloves, celery, carrots, onion, green pepper and parsley sprigs.
- Put on the lid and place the pot in the oven. Let it cook for 3 h 10 min.
- Drain the roast and shred it. Drain the veggies and finely chop them. Stir them back into the pot with the shredded roast.
- add the noodles with a pinch of salt and pepper. Put on the lid and place the pot in the oven. Let it cook for 35 min.
- Serve your stew hot warm.
- Enjoy.

Servings Per Recipe: 12

Timing Information:

Preparation	30 mins
Total Time	4 hrs. 30 mins

Nutritional Information:

Calories	450.1
Fat	23.9g
Cholesterol	110.1mg
Sodium	319.3mg
Carbohydrates	30.5g
Protein	26.7g

* Percent Daily Values are based on a 2,000 calorie diet.

Tropical Jell-O Salad

Ingredients

- 1 (3 oz.) packet orange Jell-O
- 1 tsp sugar
- 1 C. boiling water
- 1 C. cold water
- 1/2 C. carrot, peeled and shredded
- 1/2 C. canned crushed pineapple, drained

Directions

- Get a casserole dish: Stir in it the Jell-O with sugar and boiling water. Whisk them for 3 min.
- Add the cold water to the mix. Place the dish in the fridge and let it sit for 42 min.
- Lay the shredded carrots and pineapple over the Jell-O without stirring it. Place it in the fridge for at least 1 h then serve it.
- Enjoy.

Servings Per Recipe: 4

Timing Information:

| Preparation | 10 mins |
| Total Time | 10 mins |

Nutritional Information:

Calories	100.6
Fat	0.0g
Cholesterol	0.0mg
Sodium	111.3mg
Carbohydrates	24.1g
Protein	1.9g

* Percent Daily Values are based on a 2,000 calorie diet.

Cheesy Potato Casserole

Ingredients

- 8 C. raw potatoes, shredded
- 2 C. uncooked elbow macaroni
- 2 C. frozen peas
- 2 C. cooked ham
- 3 tsp salt
- 1/2 C. onion, chopped
- 4 C. cheese, shredded
- 2 quarts milk

Directions

- Before you do anything, preheat the oven to 325 F. Grease casserole dish and place it aside.
- Lay the shredded potato in the casserole then top it with the macaroni, peas, ham, salt, onion, cheese and milk.
- Place the casserole in the oven and let it cook for 2 h 35 min. Serve it hot.
- Enjoy.

Servings Per Recipe: 15

Timing Information:

| Preparation | 10 mins |
| Total Time | 2 hrs. 40 mins |

Nutritional Information:

Calories	362.7
Fat	15.6g
Cholesterol	54.4mg
Sodium	857.9mg
Carbohydrates	36.1g
Protein	19.5g

* Percent Daily Values are based on a 2,000 calorie diet.

Coconut Pudding

Ingredients

- 2/3 C. cracker crumb
- 1/2 C. sugar
- 1 tbsp flour
- 1/2 C. coconut
- 1/2 tsp salt
- 2 1/2 C. sweet milk

Directions

- Place a heavy saucepan over medium heat. Stir in it the cracker crumb with sugar, flour, coconut and salt.
- Stir into it 1/2 C. of milk. let them sit for a while.
- Heat the remaining milk. Add it to the mix and let them cook for 18 to 22 min while stirring all the time.
- Serve your pudding warm.
- Enjoy.

Servings Per Recipe: 5

Timing Information:

| Preparation | 15 mins |
| Total Time | 35 mins |

Nutritional Information:

Calories	271.1
Fat	9.7g
Cholesterol	12.2mg
Sodium	288.8mg
Carbohydrates	41.1g
Protein	6.1g

* Percent Daily Values are based on a 2,000 calorie diet.

Rolled Walnuts Tart

Ingredients

- 1 (8 inch) unbaked pie shells
- 1/2 C. butter, melted
- 3/4 C. brown sugar
- 2 eggs
- 3/4 C. light corn syrup
- 3/4 C. rolled oats
- 1/2 C. walnut pieces

Directions

- Before you do anything, preheat the oven to 350 F. Grease a pie dish and lay the pie shell in it then place it aside.
- Get a large mixing bowl: Beat in it the sugar with melted butter until they become smooth.
- Add to them the eggs with corn syrup, oats and walnuts. Pour the filling into the pie shell.
- Place the pie in the oven and let it cook for 1 h. Allow it to cool down completely then serve it with your favorite toppings.
- Enjoy.

Servings Per Recipe: 6

Timing Information:

Preparation	10 mins
Total Time	1 hr 10 mins

Nutritional Information:

Calories	621.8
Fat	32.9g
Cholesterol	111.1mg
Sodium	308.5mg
Carbohydrates	79.9g
Protein	7.0g

* Percent Daily Values are based on a 2,000 calorie diet.

Allspice Tart

Ingredients

PIE

- 3 large egg yolks
- 4 tbsp all-purpose flour
- 1 C. brown sugar, packed
- 1/8 tsp salt
- 1 tsp ground allspice
- 1/4 tsp mace
- 1/4 C. cider vinegar
- 2 C. warm water
- 1/4 C. butter, softened
- 1 (9 inch) baked pie crusts

MERINGUE TOPPING

- 3 large egg whites
- 1/4 tsp salt
- 1 tsp cider vinegar
- 6 tbsp granulated sugar
- 1 1/2 tsp cornstarch

Directions

- Before you do anything, preheat the oven to 325 F. Grease a pie dish and lay the pie crust in it then place it aside. Place a bowl on a double boiler. Whisk in it the egg yolks until they become pale.
- Add to them the flour, sugar, salt and spices. Mix them well. Stir in the vinegar and warm water.
- Let the mixture cook for 26 min over simmering water until the batter becomes thick.
- Once the time is up, stir the butter into the batter until it melts. Let it cook for an extra 18 min. Once the time is up, spoon the mix into the pie crust. Place it aside to lose heat.
- Get a large mixing bowl: Cream in it the egg whites, salt and vinegar until its soft peaks.
- Mix into it the sugar gradually by 1 tbsp at a time followed by the cornstarch while maintaining the soft peak.
- Spoon the mix over the tart filling. Place it in the oven and let it cook for 7 to 9 min.
- Allow the tart to lose heat completely then serve it. Enjoy.

Servings Per Recipe: 6

Timing Information:

| Preparation | 15 mins |
| Total Time | 50 mins |

Nutritional Information:

Calories	466.5
Fat	20.0g
Cholesterol	125.2mg
Sodium	404.0mg
Carbohydrates	67.1g
Protein	5.6g

* Percent Daily Values are based on a 2,000 calorie diet.

Glazed Crisco Puffs

Ingredients

- 9 C. cake flour
- 1 tsp salt
- 3 C. Crisco shortening
- 2 tbsp sugar
- 2 C. water

GLAZE

- 4 lbs. powdered sugar
- 1/4 C. cornstarch
- 3 tbsp evaporated milk
- 1/2 tsp vanilla
- 1 1/4 C. water

Directions

- Get a large mixing bowl: Combine in it the cake flour with salt, sugar and water until you get a dough.
- Roll the dough on a lightly floured surface. Cut it into circles of the size you desire. Place a 1 tbsp of the filling you want on the side of each circle.
- Pull the dough over the filling and press the edges to seal them.
- Place a deep pan over medium heat. Melt in it the shortening. Cook in it the puffs until they become golden brown.
- Drain them and place them aside.
- Get a mixing bowl: Mix in it the powdered sugar with cornstarch, milk, vanilla and water to make the glaze.
- Drizzle the glaze over the puffs then serve them.
- Enjoy.

Servings Per Recipe: 1

Timing Information:

Preparation	30 mins
Total Time	35 mins

Nutritional Information:

Calories	431.1
Fat	15.7g
Cholesterol	0.3mg
Sodium	60.9mg
Carbohydrates	70.7g
Protein	2.6g

* Percent Daily Values are based on a 2,000 calorie diet.

Valentine Strawberry Amish Bread

Ingredients

- 1 1/2 C. Amish starter
- 3 eggs
- 1/2 C. oil
- 1/2 C. applesauce
- 1/2 C. buttermilk
- 2 (1/3 oz.) box sugar-free strawberry gelatin mix
- 1/4 C. sugar
- 2 C. flour
- 1 1/2 tsp baking powder
- 1/2 tsp baking soda
- 1/2 tsp salt
- 1 1/2 C. sliced strawberries
- 1 tbsp sugar

Directions

- Before you do anything, preheat the oven to 325 F. Grease 5 small bread pans and place them aside.
- Get a large mixing bowl: Whisk in it the Amish starter with eggs, oil, applesauce, and buttermilk well.
- Get a mixing bowl: Add to it the gelatin mix with sugar, flour, baking powder, baking soda, and salt. Mix them well.
- Get another mixing bowl: Stir in it the strawberries with 1 tbsp of sugar. Fold it into the batter.
- Pour the batter into the greased pan. Place them in the oven and let them cook for 48 min.
- Allow the bread pans to cool down completely then serve them.
- Enjoy.

Servings Per Recipe: 10

Timing Information:

Preparation	15 mins
Total Time	1 hr

Nutritional Information:

Calories	239.7
Fat	12.8g
Cholesterol	63.9mg
Sodium	287.4mg
Carbohydrates	26.8g
Protein	5.3g

* Percent Daily Values are based on a 2,000 calorie diet.

Spicy Orange Bread

Ingredients

- 1 1/2 C. Amish starter
- 3 eggs
- 1/2 C. oil
- 1/2 C. applesauce
- 1/2 C. orange juice
- 1 (1/3 oz.) box sugar-free orange Jell-O mix
- 1/2 C. sugar
- 2 C. flour
- 1 1/2 tsp baking powder
- 1/2 tsp baking soda
- 1 1/2 tsp allspice
- 1/2 tsp cinnamon
- 1/2 tsp salt
- 1 C. dried cranberries
- 1 tbsp orange zest
- 1 C. pecans

Directions

- Before you do anything, preheat the oven to 350 F. Grease 5 small bread pans and place them aside.
- Get a large mixing bowl: Whisk in it the starter with eggs, oil, applesauce, and orange juice.
- Mix in it the orange Jell-O with flour, sugar, baking powder, baking soda, allspice, cinnamon and salt.
- Fold into them the cranberries with orange zest and pecans. Pour the batter into the pans. Cook them in the oven for 48 min.
- Allow them to cool down completely then serve them.
- Enjoy.

Servings Per Recipe: 15

Timing Information:

Preparation	20 mins
Total Time	1 hr 10 mins

Nutritional Information:

Calories	179.8
Fat	8.4g
Cholesterol	42.3mg
Sodium	172.8mg
Carbohydrates	23.2g
Protein	3.1g

* Percent Daily Values are based on a 2,000 calorie diet.

POPPY BREAD

Ingredients

- 1 C. hot water
- 1 C. Amish starter
- 1 tbsp oil
- 2 tbsp brown sugar
- 2 tsp salt
- 2 C. bread flour
- 1 1/2 C. wheat flour
- 2 tsp active dry yeast

MULTIGRAIN MIX

- 1 tbsp rye flakes
- 1 tbsp wheat flakes
- 1 tbsp whole oat groats
- 1 tbsp millet
- 1 tbsp flax seed
- 1 tbsp poppy seed
- 1 tbsp sesame seeds
- 1 tbsp sunflower seeds

Directions

- Combine all the ingredients in a bread machine by following the instructions of the manufacturer.
- Select the French bread setting and let it cook.
- Enjoy.

Servings Per Recipe: 12

Timing Information:

| Preparation | 10 mins |
| Total Time | 3 hrs. 40 mins |

Nutritional Information:

Calories	160.7
Fat	3.1g
Cholesterol	0.0mg
Sodium	391.1mg
Carbohydrates	28.7g
Protein	5.2g

* Percent Daily Values are based on a 2,000 calorie diet.

Splenda Muffins

Ingredients

- cooking spray
- 3/4 C. yellow cornmeal
- 1/4 tsp salt
- 1/2 tsp baking soda
- 1 tbsp Splenda artificial sweetener
- 1 egg, beaten
- 3/4 C. milk
- 1/2 C. Amish starter
- 2 tbsp butter, melted

Directions

- Before you do anything, preheat the oven to 375 F. Grease 12 C. muffin tin and place it aside.
- Get a large mixing bowl: Mix in it the cornmeal, salt, baking soda and Splenda.
- Get another mixing bowl: Whisk in it the eggs, milk, starter and melted butter. Add to them the cornmeal mix while stirring them all the time.
- Pour the batter into the greased muffin tin. Place it in the oven and let it cook for 40 to 50 min.
- Allow them to cool down completely then serve them.
- Enjoy.

Servings Per Recipe: 12

Timing Information:

Preparation	40 mins
Total Time	1 hr

Nutritional Information:

Calories	60.4
Fat	3.1g
Cholesterol	24.8mg
Sodium	130.4mg
Carbohydrates	6.6g
Protein	1.6g

* Percent Daily Values are based on a 2,000 calorie diet.

Nutty Carrot Muffins

Ingredients

- 3/4 C. Amish starter
- 1 egg, beaten
- 1/2 C. buttermilk
- 1/2 C. pureed sweet potato
- 1 tsp vanilla
- 1/2 C. fiber cereal
- 1/2 C. oats
- 1 tsp salt
- 2 tbsp Splenda artificial sweetener
- 1 tbsp brown sugar
- 1 1/2 C. flour
- 1 tsp baking soda
- 1/2 C. shredded carrot
- 1/2 C. raisins
- 1/2 C. chopped walnuts

Directions

- Before you do anything, preheat the oven to 375 F. Grease 12 C. muffin pan and place it aside.
- Get a large mixing bowl: Cream in it the starter with vanilla, egg, sweet potato, and buttermilk.
- Mix in the cereal with oats, salt, Splenda, brown sugar, flour, and baking soda. Fold the carrot with raisins and walnuts into the batter.
- Pour the batter into the muffin pan. Place it in the oven and let it cook for 25 to 30 min.
- Allow them to cool down completely then serve them.
- Enjoy.

Servings Per Recipe: 14

Timing Information:

Preparation	10 mins
Total Time	30 mins

Nutritional Information:

Calories	132.2
Fat	3.7g
Cholesterol	15.4mg
Sodium	276.9mg
Carbohydrates	21.3g
Protein	3.9g

* Percent Daily Values are based on a 2,000 calorie diet.

Juniper Stir Fry

Ingredients

- 1/4 C. walnut oil
- 1 tbsp white mustard seeds
- 1 medium onion, sliced
- 1 C. chicken stock
- 1 lb. sauerkraut, drained
- 1 1/2 tbsp ginger, minced
- 7 -8 juniper berries
- 1 1/2 tbsp red bell peppers, chopped

Directions

- Place a heavy saucepan over medium heat. Heat the oil in it. Stir in the mustard seeds and cook them for 40 sec.
- Mix in the onion and let it cook for 12 min over low heat with the lid on. Mix in the stock, sauerkraut, ginger, and juniper berries.
- Put on the lid and let them cook for 60 min. Serve your stir fry with bell pepper.
- Enjoy.

Servings Per Recipe: 6

Timing Information:

Preparation	10 mins
Total Time	1 hr 20 mins

Nutritional Information:

Calories	130.8
Fat	10.3g
Cholesterol	1.2mg
Sodium	558.4mg
Carbohydrates	8.2g
Protein	2.4g

* Percent Daily Values are based on a 2,000 calorie diet.

Hot Cornmeal

Ingredients

- 3 C. water
- 1 C. cornmeal
- 1 tsp salt

Directions

- Grease a baking pan and place it aside.
- Place a large saucepan over medium heat. Stir in the water with cornmeal and salt. Put on the lid and let it cook for 15 to 20 min or until it is done.
- Pour the mixture into the greased pan. Place it aside let it sit unit it lose heat completely. Slice it into squares.
- Place a large pan over medium heat. Heat in it a splash of oil. Cook in it the corn squares until they become golden brown then serve them.
- Enjoy.

Servings Per Recipe: 8

Timing Information:

Preparation	5 mins
Total Time	25 mins

Nutritional Information:

Calories	55.2
Fat	0.5g
Cholesterol	0.0mg
Sodium	298.6mg
Carbohydrates	11.7g
Protein	1.2g

* Percent Daily Values are based on a 2,000 calorie diet.

Green Stew Pan

Ingredients

- 6 slices bacon
- 3 medium onions, sliced
- 1 lb. fresh green beans, cleaned and cut into small pieces
- 2 C. fresh diced tomatoes
- 1 tsp salt
- 1/2 tsp pepper
- 1/3 C. boiling water

Directions

- Place a large pan over medium heat. Cook in it the bacon until it become crisp.
- Stir in the onion and let it cook for 10 min while stirring it often. Add the green beans and cook them for 4 min.
- Stir in the tomato with water, salt and pepper. Lower the heat and let them cook for 10 min until the veggies are done. Serve it warm.
- Get a large mixing bowl:
- Allow it to cool down completely then serve it with your favorite toppings.
- Enjoy.

Servings Per Recipe: 6

Timing Information:

Preparation	20 mins
Total Time	50 mins

Nutritional Information:

Calories	173.4
Fat	10.4g
Cholesterol	15.4mg
Sodium	771.7mg
Carbohydrates	16.7g
Protein	5.2g

* Percent Daily Values are based on a 2,000 calorie diet.

Creamy Jell-O and Egg Salad

Ingredients

- 8 oz. cream cheese, softened
- 1 C. celery, cut
- 1 C. cucumber, cut
- 1 small onion, cut
- 3 eggs, hard-boiled, cut
- 3 tbsp mayonnaise
- 3 oz. lemon Jell-O gelatin

Directions

- Get a large mixing bowl: Toss in it the celery, cucumber and onion.
- Get another mixing bowl: Mix in it 1 C. of boiling water with Jell-O. Place it aside to cool down.
- Get a small mixing bowl: beat in it the mayonnaise with cream cheese until it become smooth. Add it to the veggies with Jell-O and a pinch of salt.
- Toss them to coat. Place the salad in the fridge and let it sit until ready to serve.
- Enjoy.

Servings Per Recipe: 16

Timing Information:

Preparation	10 mins
Total Time	1 hr 10 mins

Nutritional Information:

Calories	97.9
Fat	6.8g
Cholesterol	55.9mg
Sodium	104.7mg
Carbohydrates	6.7g
Protein	2.8g

* Percent Daily Values are based on a 2,000 calorie diet.

Chicken Farm Soup

Ingredients

- 12 C. water
- 2 lbs. boneless skinless chicken breasts, cubed
- 1 C. chopped onion
- 1 C. chopped celery
- 1 C. shredded carrot
- 3 chicken bouillon cubes
- 2 (14 3/4 oz.) cans cream-style corn
- 2 C. uncooked egg noodles
- 1/4 C. butter
- 1 tsp salt
- 1/4 tsp pepper

Directions

- Place a large pot over medium heat. Stir in it the water, chicken, onion, celery, carrots and bouillon.
- Cook them until they start boiling. Lower the heat and let them cook for 35 min.
- Once the time is up, add the corn, noodles and butter to the pot. Let them cook for 12 min.
- Adjust the seasoning of the soup then serve it hot.
- Enjoy.

Servings Per Recipe: 16

Timing Information:

Preparation	15 mins
Total Time	55 mins

Nutritional Information:

Calories	153.7
Fat	4.1g
Cholesterol	44.6mg
Sodium	505.8mg
Carbohydrates	14.8g
Protein	15.0g

* Percent Daily Values are based on a 2,000 calorie diet.

Creamy Chicken Roast

Ingredients

- 1 cut-up roasting chicken
- 1/2 C. flour
- 1 tsp salt
- 1 dash pepper
- 3 tbsp butter
- 1 1/2 C. cream

Directions

- Before you do anything, preheat the oven to 350 F.
- Get a large mixing bowl: Stir in it the flour, salt, and pepper.
- Place a large pan over medium heat. Heat the butter in it until it melts.
- Dust the chicken pieces with the flour mix then cook them in the melted butter until they become golden brown.
- Drain them and transfer them to a baking pan. Drizzle the cream all over the chicken pieces. Cook them in the oven for 2 h.
- Serve your creamy chicken roast hot.
- Enjoy.

Servings Per Recipe: 6

Timing Information:

| Preparation | 20 mins |
| Total Time | 1 hr 50 mins |

Nutritional Information:

Calories	368.8
Fat	32.0g
Cholesterol	117.2mg
Sodium	492.0mg
Carbohydrates	9.7g
Protein	10.8g

* Percent Daily Values are based on a 2,000 calorie diet.

Applesauce Muffins

Ingredients

- 1 1/2 C. boiling water
- 1 tsp baking soda
- 1 C. dark molasses
- 3 C. flour
- 1 C. brown sugar, packed
- 1/4 C. butter
- 1/4 C. unsweetened applesauce

Directions

- Before you do anything, preheat the oven to 350 F. line up a muffin pan with Cake liners.
- Get a large mixing bowl: Stir in the boiling water with soda. Stir in the molasses and place it aside.
- Get a mixing bowl: Mix in in it the flour, brown sugar and margarine until you get a crumbly mix. Place 1 C. of it aside.
- Add the applesauce the rest of the crumble mix and combine them well. Pour the batter into the muffin C. Top it with the remaining 1 C. of crumbs.
- Place the pan in the oven and let it cook for 22 to 26 min.
- Enjoy.

Servings Per Recipe: 1

Timing Information:

Preparation	20 mins
Total Time	45 mins

Nutritional Information:

Calories	150.4
Fat	2.0g
Cholesterol	5.0mg
Sodium	77.8mg
Carbohydrates	31.7g
Protein	1.6g

* Percent Daily Values are based on a 2,000 calorie diet.

Vanilla Coffee Cake

Ingredients

- 2 C. light brown sugar
- 2 C. all-purpose flour
- 3/4 C. shortening
- 1 egg
- 2 tsp vanilla extract
- 1 C. hot strong coffee
- 1 tsp baking soda

Directions

- Before you do anything, preheat the oven to 325 F. Grease a cake pan and place it aside.
- Get a large mixing bowl: Combine it the sugar, flour and shortening until they become crumbly.
- Stir the baking soda into the coffee. Pour it into the flour bowl and mix them well.
- Mix in the egg and vanilla. Pour the batter into the greased pan. Place it in the oven and let it cook for 32 min.
- Allow the cake to cool down completely then serve it with your favorite toppings.
- Enjoy.

Servings Per Recipe: 6

Timing Information:

| Preparation | 10 mins |
| Total Time | 40 mins |

Nutritional Information:

Calories	671.0
Fat	26.8g
Cholesterol	35.2mg
Sodium	251.7mg
Carbohydrates	103.4g
Protein	5.4g

* Percent Daily Values are based on a 2,000 calorie diet.

Banana Cake with Vanilla Frosting

Ingredients

CAKE

- 2/3 C. vegetable shortening
- 1 2/3 C. sugar
- 3 whole eggs, room temp
- 2 1/4 C. all-purpose flour
- 1 1/4 tsp baking powder
- 1 1/4 tsp baking soda
- 1 1/4 tsp salt
- 2/3 C. buttermilk
- 1 1/4 C. bananas, mashed
- 2/3 C. chopped black walnut

PENUCHE FROSTING

- 3/4 C. butter
- 1 1/2 C. brown sugar
- 1/4 C. milk, plus
- 2 tbsp milk
- 1/2 tsp salt
- 1 1/2 tsp vanilla extract
- 3 C. powdered sugar

Directions

- Before you do anything, preheat the oven to 350 F. Grease a 2 cake pans and place them aside.
- Get a large mixing bowl: Beat in it the sugar with shortening until they become light. Beat in the eggs gradually.
- Mix in the sugar with flour, baking powder, baking soda, and salt. Add the buttermilk and combine them well until you get a smooth batter.
- Gold the banana and walnuts into the batter. Pour it into the cake pans and cook them for 36 to 42 min in the oven.
- Place a heavy saucepan over medium heat: Combine in it the brown sugar with butter until they melt. Cook them until they start boiling.
- Lower the heat and let them cook for an extra 2 to 3 min while stirring all the time. Mix in the milk and cook them until they start boiling while stirring all the time.

- Get a large mixing bowl: Pour in it the hot milk mix with vanilla and a pinch of salt.
- Add to them the powdered sugar gradually while beating them until they become smooth and creamy to make the frosting.
- Allow the cakes to cool down completely Spread the frosting all over them. Place them in the fridge until ready to serve.
- Enjoy.

Servings Per Recipe: 12

Timing Information:

| Preparation | 30 mins |
| Total Time | 1 hr 30 mins |

Nutritional Information:

Calories	700.7
Fat	28.8g
Cholesterol	78.6mg
Sodium	635.0mg
Carbohydrates	107.8g
Protein	6.4g

* Percent Daily Values are based on a 2,000 calorie diet.

Vanilla Blondies

Ingredients

- 1/4 C. butter
- 1 C. brown sugar
- 1 egg
- 1 C. all-purpose flour
- 1 tsp vanilla
- 1/2 tsp salt
- 1 tsp baking powder

Directions

- Before you do anything, preheat the oven to 350 F. Grease a cake pan and place it aside.
- Place a heavy saucepan over medium heat. Heat in it the butter until it melts. Mix in the sugar and keep stirring them until they melt.
- Turn off the heat and allow the mix to lose heat completely. Combine in the egg, flour, vanilla, salt, and baking powder. Beat them until they become smooth.
- Pour the batter into the cake pan. Cook it in the oven for 32 min.
- Allow it to cool down completely then cut it into squares. Serve your brownies or store them in the fridge.
- Enjoy.

Servings Per Recipe: 1

Timing Information:

Preparation	40 mins
Total Time	1 hr 10 mins

Nutritional Information:

Calories	222.4
Fat	6.5g
Cholesterol	41.6mg
Sodium	251.4mg
Carbohydrates	38.9g
Protein	2.4g

* Percent Daily Values are based on a 2,000 calorie diet.

Amish Mint Tea

Ingredients

- 4 quarts water, boiling
- 1 quart meadow mint tea, stems & leaves
- 4 -6 C. sugar

Directions

- Pour 4 quarts of water in a kettle. Heat them until they start boiling.
- Stir in 1 quart of tea stems and leaves. Heat them again until they start boiling.
- Once the time is up, turn the heat off and let the tea sit for 1 h while pressing it every once in a while.
- Once the time is up, discard the leaves and stems. Use a fine cheesecloth to strain the tea.
- Pour the tea in a heavy saucepan. Stir into 5 C. of sugar and heat it until it dissolves.
- Let it cool down completely then freeze it until ready to use.
- To serve your tea, Stir 1 concentrate box of it with 2 to 3 water concentrate boxes.
- Enjoy.

Servings Per Recipe: 1

Timing Information:

Preparation	15 mins
Total Time	45 mins

Nutritional Information:

Calories	309.7
Fat	0.0g
Cholesterol	0.0mg
Sodium	7.9mg
Carbohydrates	80.0g
Protein	0.0g

* Percent Daily Values are based on a 2,000 calorie diet.

Crunchy Broccoli with Cheddar Sauce

Ingredients

- broccoli
- 2 C. chopped onions
- 4 tbsp flour
- 1 tsp salt
- 2 C. milk
- 1/4 lb. mild cheddar cheese

Directions

- Before you do anything, preheat the oven to 375 F. Grease a baking pan.
- Bring a large pot of water and a pinch of salt to a boil. Stir in it the broccoli and let it cook for 8 min.
- Place a heavy saucepan over medium heat: Melt in it the butter. Add the flour and mix it well.
- Add the milk gradually while whisking all the time until you get a smooth and thick mix. Stir in the cheese until it melts to make the sauce.
- Toss half of the broccoli with onion in the baking pan. Drizzle over it half of the cheese sauce.
- Top it with the remaining half of the broccoli then drizzle the cheese sauce over it. Place the pan in the oven and let it cook for 48 min.
- Serve your broccoli casserole warm.
- Enjoy.

Servings Per Recipe: 4

Timing Information:

Preparation	10 mins
Total Time	55 mins

Nutritional Information:

Calories	252.9
Fat	14.0g
Cholesterol	46.9mg
Sodium	820.8mg
Carbohydrates	19.4g
Protein	12.7g

* Percent Daily Values are based on a 2,000 calorie diet.

Peanut Crackers

Ingredients

- 1 C. brown sugar
- 1 C. light molasses
- 1 C. water
- 1 dash salt
- 4 tbsp butter
- 2 C. shelled peanuts

Directions

- Line up and grease baking sheet.
- Place a saucepan over low heat: Stir in it the sugar, molasses, water and salt.
- Let them cook until they reach a temperature of 280 F.
- Mix in the butter until it melts. Turn off the heat and fold the peanuts into the mix.
- Pour the mix in the baking sheet. Place it aside until it cools down completely cools down and harden.
- Break it into pieces.
- Enjoy.

Servings Per Recipe: 15

Timing Information:

| Preparation | 25 mins |
| Total Time | 1 hr 25 mins |

Nutritional Information:

Calories	257.9
Fat	12.6g
Cholesterol	8.1mg
Sodium	50.0mg
Carbohydrates	34.2g
Protein	5.0g

* Percent Daily Values are based on a 2,000 calorie diet.

Sweet and Salty Beef Chili

Ingredients

- 1 lb. ground beef
- 1/2 C. chopped onion
- 1/2 C. chopped celery
- 3 tbsp flour
- 1/4 C. brown sugar
- 1/4 C. ketchup
- 4 C. tomato juice
- 2 -3 tbsp chili powder
- 16 oz. kidney beans
- salt and pepper

Directions

- Place a large pot over medium heat. Cook in it the beef, onions and celery for 8 min. Discard the excess fat.
- Mix in the flour and cook them for 2 min. Stir in the sugar with ketchup, tomato juice, chili powder, beans, a pinch of salt and pepper.
- Put on the lid and let the stew cook for 32 min. Serve it hot.
- Enjoy.

Servings Per Recipe: 6

Timing Information:

| Preparation | 30 mins |
| Total Time | 1 hr |

Nutritional Information:

Calories	326.5
Fat	12.3g
Cholesterol	51.4mg
Sodium	874.5mg
Carbohydrates	35.1g
Protein	20.3g

* Percent Daily Values are based on a 2,000 calorie diet.

Thanks for Reading! Join the Club and Keep on Cooking with 6 More Cookbooks....

http://bit.ly/1TdrStv

To grab the box sets simply follow the link mentioned above, or tap one of book covers.

This will take you to a page where you can simply enter your email address and a PDF version of the box sets will be emailed to you.

Hope you are ready for some serious cooking!

http://bit.ly/1TdrStv

Come On...
Let's Be Friends :)

We adore our readers and love connecting with them socially.

Like BookSumo on Facebook and let's get social!

Facebook

And also check out the BookSumo Cooking Blog.

Food Lover Blog

Made in the USA
Columbia, SC
17 June 2018